The Greater Miracle

The Story Behind the Story

Petrolia, Ontario, Canada

The Greater Miracle

The Story Behind the Story

By

Steve Bottrill

The Greater Miracle

The Story Behind the Story

by

Steve Bottrill

First Print Edition February 2020

ISBN: 978-1-989346-09-9

Dedication

I dedicate this book to my wife, Cat, and our children, who have always blessed me with their love and unwavering support.

Acknowledgments

First, I would like to thank God for all the blessings He has bestowed upon me: without Him, none of this is possible. He saved my life and has put the right people in place for me to succeed and spread the word.

Stacey and Pastor Kevin Weeks have given me the knowledge to develop this faith-based version of my story, without their generosity, I could not have completed this book. My thanks to them for their support.

To my publisher, Dawn Stilwell, who has put up with me and has enhanced my writing skills. Thank you.

"For I know the plans I have for you, declares the Lord, plans for welfare and not for evil, to give you a future and a hope." Jeremiah 29:11

"Pride is a black hole of consuming selfishness
at the core of fallen human nature.[1]" ~ Jon Bloom

-1-

Pride Before Destruction

Conceit drove my life, but I didn't see it as pride. I labelled it as a normal, testosterone-filled, masculine desire for respect. I hungered for wealth, but more than a number in my bank account, I yearned for the pleasure, advantages, and comforts that wealth promised. This obsession consumed me. If money brought attention, and attention gave me power, and power equalled respect, then money became the pathway to the respect I desired. I learned to navigate this path by playing nice when it benefited me, and cutthroat when it didn't.

I never prayed or even thought about praying. Unfaithful, non-religious people catapulted themselves

---

[1] Jon Bloom. "The Real Root of Sexual Sin", Desiring God, May 26 2017, https://www.desiringgod.org/articles/the-real-root-of-sexual-sin.

successfully into the world all around me. That provided enough evidence to convince my arrogant mind that I didn't need God to succeed in life. I wasn't necessarily opposed to things of faith, but if I didn't need God, why waste my time pursuing what appeared to be an endless list of rules and obligations? Besides, I couldn't reconcile the idea of a *loving God* with the evil permeating the world. I remained convinced that my choices were entirely mine and that I dictated my destiny.

The religious people I knew were fanatics, and they couldn't adequately explain criminal activity that happened behind the cloak of religion that reporters exposed. Even in our small town, headlines of religious scandal filled the local papers. I was determined to disprove the existence of God and the silliness of organized religion. I was cocky and egotistical.

Despite this ugly fixation with self, a beautiful, extroverted, God-fearing woman named Cat noticed me. She chiselled through my exterior and tunnelled her way into the softest places of my heart. Cat challenged my thinking and resolutely refused to yield to my worldview. I admired her confidence, her assurance in her beliefs, and the fact that she was drop-dead gorgeous didn't hurt. Her relaxed personality made her an enjoyable companion. She was fluent in French, which I found strangely attractive, and she shone brightest while exercising her natural gift for hospitality. People gravitated toward Cat. Despite our vast differences, we clicked. The adage proved true—opposites attract.

Religion was the greatest point of friction between us. Cat's Catholic roots ran deep, and we argued quite spectacularly about the things of God. In the back of my mind, I conceded that God existed, but I didn't want to verbalize it and be forced to deal with the life changes that must follow that admission. I had no desire to repent, turn from sin, and submit to God. Despite the differences between us, after dating Cat a week, I knew that I would one day ask her to marry me. Because selfishness drove my choices, I didn't consider how our marriage might challenge her convictions. In some ways, I didn't care. I wanted her.

Cat remained impressively unimpressed with my life's accomplishments. Years of Tae Kwon Do training took me all over the world competing at an Olympic level. I dominated on the soccer field and even considered it as a viable profession. Crowds of girls swooned over this tough athlete toying with plans to teach kindergarten, but Cat was the only girl I saw, the only one who stole my heart. On a warm summer day in August of 1995, Cat agreed to be my wife.

It was a real wake up call for me, how seriously Cat took the wedding, because she immediately started planning for the big day. She had older siblings who were already married and she knew we could not wait till the last minute to organize the wedding. I thought I might have a year to let my decision sink in but it all seemed to happen so fast.

Cat, managed the majority of our wedding details. She arranged the hall, booked the church, chose the menu, and designed the invitations. My responsibility was to show up, but I had supposed I should at least offer to help her.

I was studying at Carleton University in Ottawa, so I made as many trips as possible back home to assist Cat with our remaining wedding plans, but it was hard to find transportation. The bus was painfully slow and the train was expensive. I caught as many rides with others as I could and carted my books home with me, but studying never happened while I was home. Instead, Cat and I would dream of our future, our wedding, and how we'd manage married life while I attended Teachers' College.

Change Set in Motion

As my time at University came to a close, I planned a trip home two weeks before final exams. On March 22, 1996, I would catch a morning ride from school back home.

Early that morning, my alarm sounded. I threw on a pair of jeans and grabbed the one piece of luggage, which I had packed the previous night, and felt the cross around my neck bounce as I excitedly jumped up. Cat had given me a dark wooden cross, and I never took it off. The relic was blessed and from Medjugorje, a very religious place in Yugoslavia, and she believed it would provide me with protection. I wore it because it looked old, hung from a dark leather cowhide string, and rested over my heart. It reminded me of Cat.

I rushed downstairs so excited, almost tripping. I peeked out the front window; my ride was not there but to my shock, we were hit by a snowstorm during the night, leaving three feet of snow on the ground! It was one of those snowstorms that often occurred around the end of March. I wondered if the snowstorm was isolated to this area because there was no warning, and Cat had not said a thing about a possible snowstorm.

I rummaged through my luggage to ensure I had a change of clothes and an extra pair of socks, which I would need if the snow soaked through my shoes. I went to the window again and saw my ride in her car, parked on the side of the road with her four-way flashers blinking.

She idled against a large snow-bank that I had to scale to gain entry to the car. My stomach churned with nervousness over the treacherous trip ahead.

Once we hit the highway, I tried to relax by pulling out my music to listen to some tunes. Before I had the chance to close my eyes, an oncoming car lost control on the snow-covered road. The lady I was hitching a ride home with yanked the steering wheel to the left and then to the right, putting us into a fishtailing spin. Fortunately, she was able to steer us back to safety. We were alive, and the severity of the event left us motionless.

"Do you want to continue?" she asked.

"It's up to you." I transferred the responsibility back onto her, but I secretly hoped that she would turn around.

We continued on our journey. I put on my head-phones, reclined my seat, and fell asleep. I awoke when we reached the service-centre that was approximately one hour from Chatham. I was starving. "What time is it?" I asked.

"The drive has been extremely slow and cautious with this snowy weather, complicated by the Ontario Public Service Employees Union (OPSEU) strike." The deeply political strike had resulted in unplowed roads and highways as the OPSEU rallied against the Mike Harris government's proposed job cuts.[2]

My understanding of the strike was that it was driven by a desire for more money and greater benefits. These desires were, ironically, closely related to the same ones that drove me: a consuming need for more. Neither the government nor the strikers considered the consequences of their standoff, much like how I refused to consider the sinful roots of my passions. I refused to give time and thought to anything that might change the self-set course of my life and experienced the truth of Proverbs 14:12, ***"There is a way that seems right to a man, but its end is the way to death."***

---

[2] "Ontario Public Service Employees Union", Wikipedia, October 9 2017, https://en.wikipedia.org/wiki/Ontario_Public_Service_Employees_Union.

Author John Piper wrote of sex, money, and power, and the underlying sins that drive those passions. I don't know Piper, but in many ways, reading his words is like reading about the sin in my heart. Piper writes, "You thought you were dealing with money; paper currency and coins. But in fact, underneath you're dealing the pleasures and advantages money can buy, or the status money can signify. And then you realize, no, that's not the bottom, because underneath that is covetousness, and greed, and fear and cravings for safety or prestige or control. And then again, no, that's not the bottom either, because the Bible says that there is another reality - a condition of the heart - deeper than all those sins, and producing them like bad fruit on a bad tree.[3]"

Matthew, one of the twelve apostles who followed Jesus Christ, also wrote about the types of fruit produced by diseased trees. He writes in Matthew 7:17-20 that a healthy tree bears good fruit, but a diseased tree bears bad

---

[3] John Piper. "Money, Sex, and Power: Definitions and Foundations, Revive 2015, London", Desiring God, June 27 2015, https://www.desiringgod.org/messages/money-sex-and-power.

fruit. And then he warns us that bad fruit trees are cut down by God and thrown into the fire. I didn't know it then, but I was about to feel the fire.

"For while we were still weak, at the right time Christ died for the ungodly. For one will scarcely die for a righteous person—though perhaps for a good person one would dare even to die— but God shows his love for us in that while we were still sinners, Christ died for us."

Romans 5:6-8

A Second Chance

Out of the above verses, verse seven stands out. Maybe it's because you don't have to be a bible scholar to understand verse seven. "Perhaps, for a good person, one would dare even to die…," I understood that. Cat is a good person. I would die for her.

But this idea of God chasing me while I ran away, God pursuing me while I slighted him, God dying for me while I remained ungodly is a bit harder to understand. And somehow, twisted into God's pursuit of me, is His perfect sovereignty that allowed a horrific car accident to change everything.

God knew of my scoffing and doubt. My ridicule of him was not in secret. He knew what it would take to capture the attention of this prideful man and then he allowed it to happen. God put me in a position where I could no longer stubbornly refuse to think about Him. He forced me into a position of complete dependence.

I thought I knew what I needed in life. I believed I knew what was best for me and how to achieve it. It showed in my pursuit of Cat. I thought that I was good for her when in reality, it was Cat who was good for me. God humbled me by exposing my wisdom as foolishness. He used Cat to speak encouragement while He forced me into a position of dependence on Him. God used the hardest things in my life to bring glory to Him.

God laid me flat out, making me incapable of performing even the most basic actions. In that position of humble dependence, I had nothing left but my mind – which the accident hadn't seemed to affect at all. And through preserving my mind, God allowed me to hear a conversation between my doctor and mother that was instrumental in motivating me toward recovery.

———

"Mrs. Bottrill, your son is alive. We didn't harvest his organs as planned. We put him into a medically induced coma. We performed a tracheostomy. A ventilator is pumping oxygen to his body." His words hung in a silence that seemed to last for hours. Then, my mother inhaled a noisy breath and screamed with joy.

"When, and if, your son wakes," the doctor cautioned, "he is going to be angry that he is confined to bed. He will question why he is disabled. He will never be like he was before. He will never be 100% like you knew him. Only one in a million make it back to being 100%, back to leading a normal productive life."

The doctor's cautious optimism failed to squash my mother's joy – or my determination. A competitive spirit swept over me. It was like a surge of energy ripped through my entire body and pulsated with the desire to be better than before.

Giving up would have been easier, but I believe this fighting spirit surging through my veins was a gift from God, who up to this point, I had denied. I felt at ease, calm, and blissfully unaware of the reality and the brevity of my situation. I determined, as if it were my right to decide, that I would be that one in a million survivor.

At some point over the next ten days, Cat brought Father Mike Dwyer, her parish priest whom she had known for a long time, to visit me. He was coming to deliver my last rites that day. I'm not exactly sure when they came because I was still drifting in and out of consciousness, but I heard their conversation. Father Dwyer placed what he called a holy cross on my forehead. When the cold metal touched my skin, the medical instruments attached to my body beeped erratically. He snatched the cross off, and the instruments calmed. A few seconds later, the weight of the cross cooled my forehead again, and the machines leapt to life. Surely this was a sign? Father Dwyer then prayed for me instead of delivering last the rites as he had intended. I have no idea what it meant, but I can't deny it happened or that it encouraged Cat to believe that God was at work.

Later, as I lay there contemplating my situation, visions of Cat, my family, sporting events, victories, and times with friends flashed before my eyes. They infused me with strength and desire to return to all the beautiful things that I once loved. I peeled my eyes open. A bright and unfocused light blinded me.

"Do you know what happened to you?"

Identical male nurses, dressed from head to toe in the same clean, crisp green scrubs, peered at me. The two men moved in a surreal unison. I could see right through one of them, like a ghostly apparition.

"You've been in a coma for ten days and were in a horrific car accident." they said in unison, before merging into one person. "You can't walk or talk."

You have the wrong guy, I thought. I can get up and walk out of here right now. I tried to speak the words, but the ventilator in my throat prevented communication.

Pity filled the man's eyes. My ego hated it, so I denied his words. There was no way I had been in a coma for ten days! My pride raged. I was a good person. I followed the rules. I obeyed the Ten Commandments, (for the most part). I was nice and courteous. I tried to get along with others, and I never made fun of people, not even the people I didn't like. I lived within the boundaries of the law. By the world's standards, I was a good man who didn't deserve this. As soon as I loosened the straps that had me tethered to this bed, I would prove this guy wrong.

Once he left, I struggled against my restraints. I freed my right arm. I squirmed and slithered, wrenching my body until I freed my left arm. I shoved myself upright and dropped my feet over the edge of the bed. My bare feet thudded onto the tiled hospital floor. I would prove that man wrong. I put my body weight on my legs.

WHAM! My head slammed into the stone-cold floor. I woke up to a nurse assisting me back into bed. Why did God do this? How was this real? It didn't seem fair. There were serial criminals walking around free. Why did this happen to me and not to them?

I railed against God, as if justice demanded Him to grade me on a curve. My worldly and flawed understanding of fairness couldn't see that God owed me nothing, and it was only by His grace that I *didn't* receive what I deserved: eternal death and separation from Him.

Was I mad at God? I would have had to believe in God to be mad at Him. One half of me shouted there was no such being as God while the other half wailed at his injustices toward me. I was a paradox of emotions.

The next morning, my eyes fluttered open to find the same male nurse standing by my bed.

"In case you don't know, it's April 3rd, 1996 and you are in London, Ontario. You were in a bad car accident. You can't speak because you have a trach in your throat, and you are paralyzed from the waist down. There are several tubes in your side to help you breathe, and we stapled in a feeding tube. We have the side bed rail up to prevent you from rolling out of bed and injuring yourself. It is a miracle you are still alive!"

Did someone tell him about last night? Does he know I already fell out of bed and possibly hindered my recovery? Was that last night? I blinked my eyes trying to clear my muddled thoughts.

My ribs itched. As I adjusted to relieve the itching, the nurse explained the doctors had operated on my organs and performed emergency surgery in the middle of the night. They performed a thoracotomy. They lifted up my ribs from the side and operated on my organs because my bladder had been leaking into my stomach. The itching was a result of the stitching that closed the incision. I also suffered frontal lobe damage in my brain that had resulted in permanent eye damage, which explained my double vision.

As the days turned to weeks, and with great pain, I slowly regained the use of my limbs. As the nurses catalogued all of my injuries and explained them to me, I had to concede that it was a miracle that I was alive, and I had to consider that maybe God didn't owe me anything. Maybe God didn't deserve my earlier rant toward him.

Maybe the fact that I am even breathing was proof of His grace toward me. But that was too much to consider at this moment. I pushed the weighty thoughts aside and focused on my physical recovery.

I eventually learned to talk again. Once Cat and I could communicate, she encouraged me to pray, but I didn't know how. Cat insisted that God would give me the strength and belief to get through this and that I could speak with God like we were having a conversation. So, after she left that night, I began a dialogue with God.

Our conversations filled the endless hours of recovery. I asked God for strength to get through the difficulties of rehab while knowing full well I didn't deserve anything from him. I still didn't understand why He bothered with an arrogant man like me, but I was thankful that He did.

By focusing on the God my fiancé insisted was real, I found untapped grit and determination. I had always been a competitor and could dig deep at crucial moments of competition, but even I knew the strength building in me didn't spring from within me. I had nothing left. It took all my focus and energy just to open my eyes, but God provided me with the strength to persevere and conquer every obstacle the doctor set before me. That gave me faith to believe I would return to 100% no matter what anyone else said.

At some point, Cat brought me a magnifying glass to aid my reading. Cat had arranged some items on my bedside table that she believed would help me as I recovered. She placed a bible within my reach and seeing it every day roused a curiosity in me. I wanted to know what was written inside. Why did this book matter so much to Cat? Was it a message from God? Was it possible that I have been wrong all these years?

I picked it up, along with the magnifying glass, and opened to Jeremiah 29:11, *"For I know the plans I have for you, declares the Lord. Plans for welfare and not for evil, to give you a future and a hope."*

A boulder of emotion stuck in my throat. How was this for my welfare? How could my accident give me a future and a hope? I didn't understand, but for the first time, my lack of understanding didn't arouse anger or defiance. Instead, it stirred a desire to learn, a desire to seek to understand. I instinctively knew that understanding would come from the book in my hands. I had yet to read Proverbs 9:10, "the fear of the Lord is the beginning of wisdom," but God had placed that truth in my heart. I knew at the most basic level that I had to start with God. I knew that if I started with God, everything was going to be fine even if it had to be different. God had a plan for me.

An unexplainable peace enveloped me. I was relieved to no longer carry the weight of controlling my destiny. While bedridden in the most dependent state I have ever known, God lifted a mighty burden from my mind. I wasn't in control of my life, and I didn't need to fear this lack of control. With the removal of that weight, I was free to question everything in my life. Everything I had learned and believed up to this point was on the table being evaluated. Maybe Cat had been right all along. God is real, and He cannot be ignored forever. It was time for me to deal with my questions about God.

"When all hope seems lost, your greatest act of faith is to get yourself in front of Jesus." ~ Kevin Weeks

-3-

New Life

One night, in the middle of the night, I awoke to a beautiful blonde-haired nurse in my room. She pointed to the bible Cat had given me and asked, "Do you believe this?"

The old me would have tried to read the woman's mannerisms and facial expressions to determine what response she desired, and then tailor my reply to my benefit. But in the perpetual state of weakness and dependence in which the accident left me, I didn't have the mental energy to jump through people-pleasing, self-promoting, manipulative hoops. I simply answered from my heart, "Yes."

This was the moment God opened my eyes and moved me from disbelief to faith. I finally believed that I was no longer fighting the odds alone. I finally believed in God and understood that I needed Him.

The woman smiled a stunningly brilliant smile and left. I never saw her again. Was she a vision? A dream? A figment of my imagination? I'm not sure, but I believe that God worked at that moment to make the way clear for Him to perform the bigger miracle I stood in need of—the healing of my heart. Yes, God provided physical healing, but looking back, I rejoice that He was even more eager to do the bigger miracle of forgiving my sin. It rings amazingly similar to Mark 2:1-12 which is the bible passage from which Pastor Kevin Weeks preached on February 2nd, 2016. I summarize Weeks below:

> In Mark 2, people were cramming into Simon's house to hear Jesus speak. The house filled up and spilled out people into the surrounding area. The crowd wanted to catch a glimpse of this guy (Jesus) who has power like they had never seen before. They came to see something great, but the majority wanted to see Jesus do something *for* them not

something *in* them. And Jesus preaches the Word. He invited them not to be healed, but to be saved.

Four friends of a paralytic carried him to Simon's house. When they couldn't get into the house, they heaved their buddy up on the roof and clawed out a hole above Jesus. They lowered their friend through the roof and dropped him *right in front of Jesus*.[4]

Cat did that for me. Like the paralytic man, I had no way of getting myself to Jesus. I was dead in my sin and ignorant of my need. I wanted God to do something for me, not something in me. Like those four friends who couldn't save or heal their buddy, Cat couldn't save me. And, completely blinded by my sin, I couldn't save myself.

Cat could, however, consistently and lovingly keep bringing me to Jesus. She could ensure a bible was always within my reach. She prayed for me, and she encouraged

---

[4] Kevin Weeks. "Get to Jesus", Harvest Bible Chapel Brantford Podcast, Feb 2 2016, https://itunes.apple.com/ca/podcast/getting-to-jesus/id884093635?i=1000361817836&mt=2

me to pray for myself. She did whatever she could to drop me in front of Jesus minute after minute, hour after hour, day after day. This belief that only God could accomplish what I needed prompted her to redirect me back to Jesus tirelessly. It was the most loving thing she could do.

Weeks continues in his sermon:

When life is hard, you do whatever you can to get yourself in front of Jesus.

Jesus knows your need. Everybody knew why the paralytic was there before Jesus. Everyone knew he needed physical healing. But Jesus healed his heart (forgave him) before he healed his legs. Why? Your sin will always matter to Jesus more than your suffering. Don't misunderstand. Jesus cares about our suffering. Scripture is full of promises that remind us of how much Jesus wants to be with us, how compassionate Jesus is to us, how Jesus walks with us through our suffering. That's the hope we cling to, but the healing of your body will not save your soul. The healing of circumstances will not save you. Healing from a broken marriage will not save you. Healing from the pain of your past will not save you. The only thing that will save you is the healing of your soul that only Jesus Christ can do in you.

At this point, Jesus looks at the man (the paralytic) and says, "Son, your sins are forgiven." Mark 2:5. This really upset the scribes, who questioned Jesus' authority to forgive sins. Only God could forgive sin, and Jesus' statement was the equivalent of declaring himself to be God.

Jesus addressed this concern and said to the scribes, "Why do you question these things in your hearts? Which is easier to say to the paralytic, 'Your sins are forgiven,' or to say, 'Rise and take up your bed and walk'? But that you may know that the Son of Man has authority on earth to forgive sins"— he said to the paralytic— "I say to you, rise, pick up your bed, and go home."

The man rose and immediately picked up his bed and went out before them all so that they were all amaze. They glorified God, saying, "We never saw anything like this!" Mark 2:8-12

Jesus heals the man's heart before he heals his legs. I believe the woman I mentioned at the beginning of this chapter, the woman I saw who questioned my faith, is representative of God's desire to first heal my heart and move me from hopelessness to hopefulness.

Earthly healing, as magnificent and wonderful as it is to receive, is a dim foreshadowing of eternity where Jesus heals all wounds, rights every wrong, and welcomes the redeemed into his eternal presence. "Yes, be amazed at earthly healing," says Weeks, "but be more amazed at the Lord who heals."

After this great exchange with God, things began to change in me. I was certain that I would fully recover, and my recovery started to excel at an incredible speed. But the changes in me were not merely physical. God was growing my faith in Him.

Even today, nearly twenty years later, God continues to challenge me and bring me to a deeper understanding of my sin and a deeper understanding of Him and his ultimate power. The real story is not how God saved my physical life and then blessed me by allowing me to recover against tremendous odds. The real story is not even that He blessed me with a beautiful family and ministry to others. That can't be the real story because sometimes God's best for a person is no change in circumstance. Sometimes God's plan for a person is suffering, or hardship, or death. In no way am I implying that God's best always includes physical healing or a granting of wishes. God's ways and thoughts are higher than ours and we cannot understand them (Is 55). What I am saying is that God's best is always what's best, even if it is not what we want. I wanted physical healing, but God first gave me what I needed: spiritual healing.

Like the paralytic, the real story is the forgiveness of my sins and God's undeserving grace toward me. In great mercy, he not only opened my eyes to the reality of a spiritual realm that my former veiled eyes could not see, but he brought me to repentance and forgave my sins. These were gifts from God.

I began to more fully understand what God required from me. He required my repentance, which means I acknowledged my sin against Him and His right to judge me guilty. Then, I turned from my sin. When I turned from my sin, I turned toward Jesus and found forgiveness in Him. I benefited from Jesus' complete payment for my sin through His death, and I knew victory through His resurrection. I was born again. This too, is a gift from God.

Like the man Nicodemus, in John 3:1-15, I didn't fully understand what it meant to be born again. I knew I had a long way to go but I no longer walked in my strength or in my wisdom. I had the Holy Spirit in me. And, like the paralytic, if I was ever tempted to doubt God's ability to pay for and forgive my sins, I only had to remember His amazing work in my body. He proved His ability and authority to forgive me when he healed my physical body.

Is that how God will work in your life? I don't know. I don't know if His plan includes your physical healing, but I do know it includes your spiritual awakening. He wishes that none should perish, that all would come to repentance and faith in the only name under heaven by which we must be saved: Jesus (Acts 4:12).

When God saved my physical life, he made it possible for me to respond to His love, which would save my eternal life. He gave me a powerful testimony, to share the gospel as I share my story. I had a great physical need, and as God met that need, He proved that He could meet every need—known and unknown. He proved that He could meet our greatest need, which is salvation from our sins. I needed saving from my sin just as much as I needed saving from the tragic effects of that accident.

God allowed me to live and overcome seemingly insurmountable odds. I was a non-believer of the worst kind, and then he demonstrated His awesome power to heal physically and spiritually. If he could do it in me, the worst of sinners, he can do it in anybody.

In those early days of recovery, I was a baby in my faith reborn by the power of God. In many ways, my physical development mirrored my spiritual growth. As I learned to talk and walk again, I also began to grow in this new understanding of God. I had a passion for sharing His goodness and mercy. But before I could share my story, I had to learn to read and write again. But at this point in my recovery, I could hardly speak, let alone proclaim that Jesus Christ is Lord.

Encouraging Scripture:

James 1:5, "If any of you lacks wisdom, let him ask God, who gives generously to all without reproach, and it will be given him."

Matthew 6:25-27, "Therefore I tell you, do not worry about your life, what you will eat or what you will drink; or about your body, what you will put on. Is not life more than food, and the body more than clothing? Look at the birds of the air; they neither sow nor reap nor gather into barns, and yet your heavenly Father feeds them. Are you not of more value than they? And which of you, by being anxious, can add a single hour to his span of life?

And He who was seated on the throne said, "Behold, I am making all things new!" Revelation 21:5

5

Longing for Home

To my surprise, learning to speak again was more difficult than I expected. I knew what I wanted to say, but giving voice to those words was another matter. To further complicate things, the accident and resulting lifesaving treatment had impacted my voice, leaving me with little to no expression.

Wanting to be understood but unable to adequately express my desires frustrated me. I desperately wanted to go home, but all I could do was repeat the word 'home.' I made the request to everyone I saw. Doctors. Nurses. Visiting family. Cat. Concerned friends. They all responded with the same maddening words: *not yet*. It felt like no one was listening to me, and frustration built up inside. I wasn't able to vent my irritation because forming the needed words still eluded me.

On one particular day, while sitting at the end of the hall with my family and Cat, I said it again, "Home, home."

"No, not yet," my brother answered, predictably.

Then, my dad said something different. He said, "When you get stronger."

His words of affirmation gave me hope. They had heard me, but I had to get stronger. I decided to participate in as much physiotherapy as possible. I was determined that I would run when they asked me to walk. I would make every impossible goal possible. I would go home.

It took me months to learn to walk again and years to walk perfectly and not lose my balance. I imagine my gait looked strange and awkward in those early days, but just being upright was a victory worth celebrating. During my recreational therapy, the therapist and I would walk victory laps around the hospital campus. But walking was no longer good enough for me. I wanted to run.

I asked the therapist for permission. Nerves churned up my stomach. Would he refuse? Would he say it was too dangerous? Would he, like many others, simply tell me to be satisfied with my miraculous recovery thus far?

"Were you a runner before the accident?" he asked.

"Yes." I tensed. I knew my body was weak, but I wanted to do this. I needed to do this. "Where do you want me to meet you?" I pressed him.

"Just behind those old residential buildings." He pointed to old barracks that once housed veterans.

I started. Running uses different muscles than walking, so I didn't start fast. Nothing about my form felt graceful or smooth. I had fallen far from my former days as a star athlete, but that didn't discourage me. Once I turned the corner and moved out of the therapist's sight, I tried to slow down. Even at my sluggish pace, a controlled stop was difficult, but I couldn't maintain my speed any longer. Just ahead, the gate marked the end of the hospital grounds. My head throbbed like my brain was going to burst, but I pushed on. If I wanted to go home, I had to get stronger.

My drive and determination baffled the therapists who struggled to explain my rapid recovery with science because "no one ever recovers to 100%," they would say. They had never seen a recovery like mine. The brightest minds and most gifted specialists gave me a 3% chance of living and no chance of recovering to any quality of life, but they didn't account for God. I'd wag a stern finger at their negativity. Nothing could shake my confidence in what I believed the Lord was doing in my life and body.

It's been over twenty years since that accident, and what God started in me back then still stirs a longing. All who claim to follow the Lord Jesus Christ should have this ache. But the place for which we crave should not be a comfortable dwelling, perhaps built with a spouse and filled with children, love, and laughter. It is not a destination that can be reached by human effort and perseverance. Revelation 21 gives a tiny glimpse of the home waiting for all those who call upon the name of Jesus in repentance for salvation.

"Revelation 21 dwells on the new heaven and the new earth, the holy city prepared as a bride, where God dwells with man, and God wipes every tear from our eyes. Death will be no more, and neither shall there be mourning, nor crying, nor pain—for they have passed away.

A voice from the throne declares, *"Behold, I am making all things new."* Here, there is no need for the moon or the sun, for the glory of God gives light and its lamp is the Lamb. **All this awaits if your name is written in the Lamb's book of life.**

As the heavy decay of fallen life increases with each rotation of the earth, the blessed truth of Revelation 21 breathes fresh hope in Jesus. There will be no more tears in hospital waiting rooms or funeral homes. Loved ones will no longer pass away because death itself will pass away. All things will be new for those whose name is written in the Lamb's book of life because God says all things will be new. No matter how today ends this truth remains: *God is making all things new*."[5]

God plants a longing for this home in the heart of every believer. God used my accident and subsequent miraculous recovery to wake this longing deep inside my soul. This earth is not my home. Because of Jesus, one day I will open my eyes in the place the Lord has created for me, and this longing will fully be satisfied. I will be home when I am with Him.

Acts of Mercy

Every day that I woke up in my hospital room, I had a decision to make. I could give into the darkness that desired to snuff out the light of hope Christ had ignited in me, or I could yield my desires to God, submit my will to His, and follow wherever He led. Psalm 88 uses words to

---

[5] Stacey Weeks. "He Makes All Things New", Glorious Surrender, February 23 2017, https://staceyweeks.com/2017/02/23/he-makes-all-things-new/

describe the depression that many experience after an accident like mine.

The Psalmist uses words and phrases like:

- dead
- in the grave
- no more
- cut off
- depths
- dark
- deep
- things lay heavy and overwhelm
- we are shunned, horrified, and helpless
- we are filled with sorrow and cannot escape
- wrath, destruction, and darkness abound

The psalmist questions God in his despair. He acknowledges the sovereignty that allows the trial: 'You (God) have caused' and 'Your wrath.' But implied throughout the psalm is the understanding that the God who allows sorrow is the same God who brings the victory. Unlike most other psalms, this lament does not build to a conclusion of confident joy and praise. This one ends in pain. The victory has yet to come. Hope has yet to burst through the clouds, making this psalm resonate deeply with those still waiting. Despite the Psalmist's grief, he does not forget with whom his hope remains.

> Lord, he writes,
> God of my salvation.
> I call upon you, O Lord.
> I spread my hands before You.
> I cry out to You.
> My prayers come before You.

Our hope, in the darkest of grief and in the unrelenting pain of delays, is in the Lord."[6]

---

6 Stacey Weeks. "When the Grief is Deep and Hope is Dim", April 20 2017, https://staceyweeks.com/2017/04/20/when-the-grief-is-deep-and-hope-is-dim/

I faced tremendous pressure to accept the miraculous recovery I had experienced as finished. Instead, I chose to keep fighting. Culture screamed that if I looked deep within myself, I would find everything I needed to succeed. But when I looked deep within, I only saw what I lacked. I saw a man who had run from God, who had lived proudly and separated himself from depending on anyone or anything. If I was going to recover, I needed to silence the outside voices and look beyond me. I needed the Lord. I needed to remember what the psalmist wrote: ***My hope is in the Lord.***

When I focused on God, not on me, I saw every step of my recovery as a call to repent, to turn from sin, and embrace the forgiveness of God. God was asking me to listen to His voice, not the voice of others. He was asking me to depend on Him, not me. He was asking me to move from simply being aware of the Lord to completely surrendering all that I am and all that I have to Him to use for His purposes and glory.

But this call went even further. God didn't save me so I could be comfortable in this life. In 1 Peter 2:9, the apostle Peter writes that God has called us to, ***"proclaim the excellencies of him who called you out of darkness and into his marvelous light.*"** The world is filled with people who need to hear of Jesus and **"*how will they call on him in whom they have not believed? And how are they to believe in him of whom they have never heard? And how are they to hear without someone preaching*?"** (Romans 10:14). **"*As each has received a gift, use it to serve one another, as good stewards of God's varied grace*"** 1 Peter 4:10.

This has given my life new meaning. I pledged to the Lord that once I recovered, I would help others. I want to encourage those who have experienced a life-altering event to resist the negative voices and to resist looking within for courage. I want to encourage them to turn to and depend on the Lord even if their victory is yet to come, even if hope has yet to burst through the clouds.

My accident was a second chance that moved me off a wide and easy path that leads to eternal suffering onto the narrow and harder path that leads to eternal life. For that, I praise the Lord.

"I have been crucified with Christ. It is no longer I who live, but Christ who lives in me. And the life I now live in the flesh I live by faith in the Son of God, who loved me and gave himself for me." ~ Galatians 2:20

6

Live by Faith

My accident changed everything. God grabbed hold of me and set my feet on a new path. I am living proof of Proverbs 16:9, ***"The heart of man plans his way, but the Lord establishes his steps.***"

I had planned my course. I was getting married and going to conquer the business world the same way I conquered the competitive sports world—through grit and determination. Then, God stepped in and changed everything. When he brought me from spiritual death to spiritual life, I ceased to live for myself. The old me died in that crash. The new me lives to proclaim Christ.

Although certain of this new calling on my life, I still feel strangely insecure. Would people believe my story? Do I have any authority to speak into the life of another person? But no matter how many doubts rise within, I know I want to be a messenger of God. I need to tell of His greatness and kindness toward me and give hope and strength to the hopeless. And when I feel overwhelmed and unsure, I need only to read the last half of Galatians 2:20, ***"…I live by faith in the Son if God, who loved me and gave himself for me***." God's love is my fuel.

This new faith, although fragile and immature in many ways, is changing my life. My life's purpose is no longer about how I can make the most money, how I can become the most powerful man in the room, or how I can manipulate circumstances to go my way. My purpose has been wonderfully simplified. I want what God wants.

But sometimes, we talk like discovering God's will for our lives is complicated. We act like it is a big mystery only the most scholarly mind is able to discern. But Scripture is clear about God's will for believers. This is not an exhaustive list of verses about God's will for his children, but I pray these verses will, in some ways, simplify the topic for you.

- **God wants us to know him through faith in Jesus Christ.** *1 Timothy 2:4-6, "Who desires all people to be saved and to come to the knowledge of the truth. For there is one God, and there is one mediator between God and men, the man Christ Jesus, who gave himself as a ransom for all, which is the testimony given at the proper time."*

- **God's will is for us to be thankful.** *1 Thessalonians 5:18, "Give thanks in all circumstances, for this is the will of God in Christ Jesus for you."*

- **God's will is for us to do good.** *1 Peter 2:15, "For this is the will of God, that by doing good you should put to silence the ignorance of foolish people."*

- **God's will is for us to be transformed and different from this world.** *Romans 12:2, "Do not be conformed to this world, but be transformed by* *the renewal of your mind, that by testing you may discern what is the will of God, what is good and acceptable and perfect. "*

- **God wishes that none would perish, but all would know him**. *2 Peter 3:9, "The Lord is not slow to fulfill his promise as some count slowness, but is patient toward you, not wishing that any should perish, but that all should reach repentance."*

- **God desires us to be fair, kind, and humble**. *Micah 6:8, "He has told you, O man, what is good; and what does the Lord require of you but to do justice, and to love kindness, and to walk humbly with your God?"*

- **God wants us to trust him and continue doing good even when it is difficult.** *1 Peter 4:19, "Therefore let those who suffer according to God's will entrust their souls to a faithful creator while doing good.*

- **God wants to sanctify us**. *1 Thessalonians 4:3-8 "For this is the will of God, your sanctification: that you abstain from sexual immorality, that each one of you know how to control his own body in holiness and honor, not in the passion of lust like the Gentiles who do not know God; that no one transgress and wrong his brother in this matter, because the Lord is an avenger in all these things, as we told you beforehand and solemnly warned you. For God has not called us for impurity, but in holiness. Therefore, whoever disregards this, disregards not man but God, who gives his Holy Spirit to you."*

What does all that mean? It means it is God's will that you would know Him and love him. It is God's will that you are a thankful and humble person who acts kindly, justly and humbly in all circumstances. It is God's will that you are different from this world and that you are transformed by a new mind. It is God's will that none should perish, that you would entrust your soul to your faithful God as he sanctifies you. Sanctifies is a fancy way of saying that although God has made His children holy through the finished work of Jesus, we must obey His word and mature in our faith in a way that sets us apart from the world.

These truths give my life purpose. Money is no longer the ultimate goal, rather helping others change their lives for the better is the ultimate goal.

Believe it or not, my life took a turn for the better after that accident. If not for that state of desperation, my heart might still be hard and selfish. Those dependent days and nights when God met each need and gave me incredible strength, energy, and an overwhelming sense of well being, leave me with no doubt I am alive today because of God.

I desire to honour Him and proclaim Him. I believe this book is only one way that God is using my story to spread His message of hope. It is crazy to think, but yes, God is everything He says in the bible and more! There is so much more to Him that our brains can comprehend, we haven't even begun to scratch the surface of His awesome power. God is all-powerful, and anything is possible with Him. The hopeless can find hope and salvation.

Now, I work at the VON as an exercise therapist, helping senior citizens and people with disabilities stay healthy and strong and lead a better quality of life. I am the specialty fitness coordinator for southern Ontario for the VON. I help people with Multiple Sclerosis, Parkinson's, and victims of brain injuries and strokes stay healthy and strong through exercise.

I am a frequent guest speaker at schools and churches and a regular contributor to the Chatham-Kent television show, Live Your Purpose, where I feature people in Chatham Kent that are making a positive difference. I live Proverbs 3:5-6. ***I trust in the Lord with all my heart. I no longer depend on my understanding. Instead, I acknowledge Him and all He has done and trust that He will make my path straight.***

I don't know where God has taken you. You might be in a difficult place where you don't want to hear or consider God's plan for you in your suffering. I do understand that. I once lived there too. But hear this word: your feelings do not remove His call on your life. I was given the gift of life to share my story with the world and give new hope to all. I am not alone in this call.

Will you answer His call?

From Steve

A sincere thank you to everyone that helped me to realize that God is always with me and that I just need to ask for His help and guidance to get through anything.

Anything is possible with God by your side. If you would like me to pray for you and add you to my prayer circle, I would love to hear from you. We are stronger when we join our voices. My email address is:
scbottrill@gmail.com.